P9-EDM-442

Ron Wilson
Vanishing Species

CHARTWELL BOOKS INC.

Designed and produced by
Albany Books
36 Park Street London W1Y 4DE

First published 1979

Published by Chartwell Books Inc.
A Division of Book Sales Inc.
110 Enterprise Avenue
Secaucus, New Jersey 07094

Copyright © Albany Books 1979

Printed in Hong Kong

All rights reserved. No part of this
publication may be reproduced, stored
in a retrieval system or transmitted in
any form or by any means, electronic,
mechanical, photocopying, recording or
otherwise, without the prior permission
of the copyright owner

Design: Ann Houlgate
Picture research: Mary Corcoran

Endpapers: *Indian elephants.* (Aquila
Photographics, N. Jagannathan)

Title page: *Polecat.* (Eric Hosking)

Opposite: *Once common in the British Isles,
the wild cat is now found only on the
Scottish mainland.* (NHPA, R. Balharry)

Contents

Introduction

It was almost certainly a disastrous day for many of the wild animals which roamed the earth at the time that 'modern' man appeared. For, with his advanced brain and modern methods of farming and living, the fate of many species was sealed. Extinction was relatively close at hand, not only for those species which had a distinctly limited distribution, but also for many common birds, animals and insects. Of course the destruction did not happen over night, but was a gradual process.

Today, sayings like 'as dead as a dodo', now assimilated into our everyday language, mean very little to most people. And yet the dodo is one of the birds which have suffered because of man's greed. The dodo was added to the list of extinct species within a very short time of its discovery. The bird, large and flightless, was first discovered by sailors on the Indian Ocean island of Mauritius when they landed there in the 16th century. Ever on the lookout for food, they killed the bird, finding it particularly palatable. Within 150 years, there were no more dodos.

No one is really certain how many of these birds there were in the first place. But if the information about the dodos is vague, the story of the American passenger pigeon is much better documented. It was noted that, in 1871, one colony alone consisted of 136 million of these birds, It took just forty-two years to exterminate *all* America's passenger pigeons.

The history books tell us that even before man had set foot on the planets, some species had already become extinct. Those which are normally termed dinosaurs readily spring to mind. It seems likely that during the natrual course of evolution, these large animals were no longer able to survive the changing environmental conditions, and so they perished — not at the hand of man, but through the process of natural selection.

Today's story is rather different. In the last 2000 years, as man has been seen to advance, more and more animals have either become endangered species or have actually reached the point of extinction. During that time, it has been estimated that 200 species have gone the same way as the dodo and the passenger pigeon: most have become extinct in the last 100 years. This large number only includes larger animals, like birds and mammals, and it seems probable that vast numbers of invertebrates have also perished.

Land animals are not the only ones to become threatened. Many animals which spend their lives in the seas and oceans of the world are also in danger. The whales are a classic example and, in spite of definite evidence which suggests that if whaling continues there will soon be no more to hunt, many countries still continue the slaughter almost unabated.

Man has become more conscious of the need for conservation, and in one or two instances it has been possible to reverse the trend. Some species, like the nene and Swinhoe's pheasant, have been

able to increase in numbers as a result of deliberate breeding programmes.

Despite these limited successes, the future is still very bleak for many species; it has even been suggested by some authorities that some common species, such as the British robin, will have disappeared by the end of this century. If this seems unlikely, one should only remember the fate of the passenger pigeon.

Within the pages of this book can be found some of the birds and mammals which are endangered species. They are but a few of those listed by organisations such as the International Union for the Conservation of Nature (IUCN), which has its headquarters in Switzerland, and the World Wildlife Fund, which has branches in many countries.

In spite of various agreements to protect rare species, like those drawn up by the IUCN, many countries, while supporting such ideas in principle, are turning a blind eye to what is really happening. Indeed, it is these countries which are bringing the name of conservation into disrepute.

Below: *The sad result of seal hunting by Eskimos in Canada.* (Spectrum)

The Americas

Puma

The wild cats, of which the puma is a member, have suffered very badly in recent years. Although many are protected in various parts of the world, the price obtained for a skin, mainly for the fashion trade, is such that it is still worth breaking the law. But it is not only its value in this field that has helped to cause its downfall. Many other wild animals on which the puma preyed have disappeared, and yet it still has to feed to survive.

Because wild animals have often been replaced with domestic stock, the puma has naturally turned its attention to this new source of food. It takes cattle, horses and sheep and has, as would be expected, become outlawed by farmers and landowners. Of the wild animals, hoofed species such as deer form the mainstay of its diet.

It has a wide range of habitat, and will be found in desert areas and high up on mountain slopes. Jungles too will also provide both home and food for this beautiful cat. Its actual status and distribution is probably not clearly known, but it is likely that it stretches from the Strait of Magellan in the south to the northwest provinces of Canada.

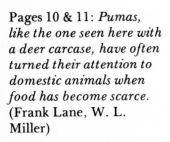

Pages 10 & 11: *Pumas, like the one seen here with a deer carcase, have often turned their attention to domestic animals when food has become scarce.* (Frank Lane, W. L. Miller)

Below: *Puma kittens.* (Frank Lane, W. L. Miller)

Chinchilla

The name chinchilla conjures up the picture of a captive animal, bred for its valuable fur. While those bred for this purpose must run into many millions, the wild animal is extremely rare. Not unlike a squirrel in general shape, the chinchilla is a rodent, which means that its teeth have evolved in such a way that it can gnaw.

Inhabiting the rocky terrain in mountainous areas of South America, from Bolivia to Chile, its numbers have drastically decreased by over-hunting. Today, conservation measures have worked in some areas and the chinchilla may be on the increase.

Its delicate, silklike, silvery-grey fur has endeared it to women for fashion garments. It lives below the ground in burrows in its mountainside home. Although it may be nocturnal in some areas, it is not strictly a night-living animal and may be seen out during the hours of daylight, where it will search out a variety of plant foods which include mosses, grasses and roots.

Right: *Inhabiting mountainous areas in South America, conservation measures have led to an increase in the once rare chinchilla.* (S. C. Bisserot)

Left: *Because careful conservation measures have been taken, the threatened extinction of the vicuna has been averted.* (NSP, Hans Dossenbach)

Vicuna

Although it is unlike the camel in shape, the vicuna belongs to the same group of animals. In South America there are four members of this family — the llama, alpaca, guanaco and vicuna. The latter is the smallest of the four and stands about 80cm (30in) at the shoulder. It is quite often mistaken for a llama, although it is less bulky in stature.

Found in several South American countries, including Bolivia, Peru, Chile and Argentina, it lives on grassland; it is grass, and other herbs, which form the main part of its diet. When alarmed and agitated, the vicuna will spit. This often consists of unpleasant semi-digested food and, as with other animals which belong to the camel family, the vicuna is quite prepared to use its teeth — particularly the lower incisors — to inflict a painful bite.

Careful conservation methods have done a great deal to increase numbers, and it is likely that it will no longer be an endangered species, although over-zealous killing for food and other useful products could once more lead to its decline.

Below: *The vicuna in its natural habitat, the high grasslands of Peru.* (NHPA, R. Perry)

Pronghorn

Although the pronghorn (or American antelope) appears to be like an antelope, it is not a true one. At one time it shared the vast American plains with the much larger American bison which, sadly, has now become extinct as a wild animal.

In spite of the fact that the pronghorn is an endangered species, it can still be seen in a number of areas, its existence due in no small measure to active conservation control. Found in the northern half of Mexico, its territory extends north to include parts of the western United States. In Canada, herds can still be seen roaming the grassy plains of the southwest.

The pronghorn has an unusual, but nevertheless effective, warning mechanism. Possessing short white hairs on its rump, it attracts the attention of fellow animals, and warns them of impending danger, by making these hairs stand on end. Because of their distinctive colour, they are extremely conspicuous and can be seen from great distances.

Although the animal has been, and probably still is, hunted, it is not easy to pursue, because it can attain speeds of 60-70 kmh (37-43 mph) which it can sustain for quite long periods. Indeed, it has the distinction of being North America's fastest animal.

The pronghorn has a number of animal enemies when it becomes incapacitated by heavy snow. It is in very cold winters that many animals succumb to the severe conditions. Unlike many other species, it does not move away to warmer climes at this time of the year.

Above: *An animal of the plains, the pronghorn antelope once shared the open spaces with the American bison.* (OSF, L. L. Rue III)

Galapagos Penguin

The Galapagos Islands will always be associated with Charles Darwin who, after spending some time there, came up with his book *The Origin of Species* which, while controversial at the time, has become an important standard reference work. Many decades later it is still considered a classic scientific study.

Because of their position and isolation, various species have evolved on the many Galapagos Islands and occur no where else in the world. One such species is the Galapagos penguin. The range of the bird is limited to two of the islands: Narborough and Albermarle.

Seeking out secluded caves close to the sea, the penguin will lay two white eggs. Although it is quite common to find eggs for much of the year, the peak laying period is May and June. The young penguins will hatch out about forty days after the eggs are laid. Like the adults they have a fish diet and until they are ready to catch their own food it is brought to them by their parents.

In recent years the Galapagos Islands have seen an influx of people. They are the sight for a new holiday industry and this, and the fact that the eggs are undoubtedly collected, has led to fears that the Galapagos penguin might become extinct.

Below: *Confined to the Galapagos Islands, the Galapagos penguin may well become extinct if tourism increases.*
(NHPA, R. Perry)

Ivory-billed Woodpecker

At one time the ivory-billed woodpecker was thought to be extinct. With the clearance of more and more forests in Cuba and the southeastern states of America, the habitat which the woodpecker had previously occupied, with very little disturbance, was disappearing rapidly; so was the number of birds. By 1920 it was assumed that the ivory-billed woodpecker could be added to the list of extinct species. Gradually, however, a number of sightings were made. Today, although it is thought that the bird still manages to survive, its position is extremely precarious.

The ivory-billed woodpecker rates as one of the three largest species of woodpecker in the world. Like other members of the family, it lives up to its name of woodpecker by 'attacking' trees to remove wood-boring insects and their larvae. Such beetles are more likely to attach themselves to older, rather than younger, trees. Thus forests with trees of varying stages of development are essential to provide a suitable supply of food for this large bird.

Southern Bald Eagle

Although the southern bald eagle is still found over a wide area of North America, with specimens occuring as far apart as northern Mexico and Alaska, it is by no means a common species. As the American national emblem, much has been done to protect it from extinction, and breeding birds occur over much of its range. Nevertheless, legislative procedures affording potential protection do not seem to be working as effectively as had been hoped and its numbers are still steadily declining.

A bird of prey, the bald eagle takes a wide variety of live food, including waterfowl, lambs, marmots, squirrels, fish and rabbits, as well as some carrion.

Opposite: *Ivory-billed woodpecker.* (Ardea, P. Morris)

Right: *A powerful bird of prey, the bald eagle, although protected by legislation, is still on the decline.* (Bruce Coleman Ltd., W. Brooks)

Trumpeter Swan

Having the distinction of being the largest of all the wildfowl to be found in North America, the trumpeter swan has declined rapidly in numbers. Yet it is sad to relate that it was sharing the earth with many other creatures nearly 300,000 years before man made his appearance. For many centuries it lived in peaceful co-existence with man until he became a hunter; bones, dated by modern radiocarbon techniques, have shown that the birds were killed at least two thousand years ago, presumably for food.

For much of its life it ranged over a large area, but as the hunters arrived in earnest in the 19th century the trumpeters became their targets and slowly declined. In most cases the decline of a species has gone unchecked until quite recently, but not so with the large and gracefully elegant trumpeter swan. The fact that it has been saved from extinction is certainly due to the creation of the Yellowstone National Park in the middle of the 19th century.

Today both Canada and the USA have laws to protect this magnificent bird, which has a length of 165cm (65in) and a wingspan of 106-138cm (42-54in). Other factors have, however, affected it, including the use of toxic chemicals on agricultural land, in marshes and along rivers.

The largest of North America's wildfowl, the trumpeter swan displays its majesty in flight and on the water. (NHPA, J. Tallon)

Europe

European Bison

The current world population of bison consists of only two species within the genus. These are the European bison and the American bison. At one time both were common animals over their respective continents. Indiscriminate killing of the American bison almost wiped out the species on that continent; similar disaster has struck the European species.

Although closely related they are animals of different habits. The European bison, with an alternative name of wisent, inhabited woodland: the American animal roamed the wide open plains. There are two European sub-species; these are the mountain (or Caucasian) bison and the lowland (or Lithuanian) bison.

The European species relies on woodland both for shelter and for food. Although large of stature, it does very little damage to the woodland vegetation, and undoubtedly much less than that caused by man and other forest-dwellers. A browsing animal, it takes its fill from the bark of such trees as poplar, lime, ash, maple, aspen and sallow. In the autumn the oak's acorns make a welcome change to the diet and provide plenty of food when there is a good crop.

As the forests of Europe were mercilessly felled, the bison's natural habitat decreased until, by the beginning of this century, there was only one herd remaining in the Polish Bialowiecza Forest, now a national park. That they had survived there for so long was due in no small measure to the fact that the herd was managed at the instigation of the Russian Imperial family.

Today the European bison has vanished as a wild species, although many have been bred in captivity and released back into the open in selected areas.

Right and pages 22 & 23: *An animal of woodland, the European bison is now only found as a captive species.* (S. C. Bisserot; NSP, P. H. Ward)

Left: *The pine marten as seen in its natural habitat of pinewoods. The stripping of pinewoods in Britain has resulted in an alarming decrease in the pine marten population.* (NHPA, R. Balharry)

Below: *The pine marten's diet is varied; here it is seen with a dead pigeon.* (Frank Lane, G. Quedens)

Pine Marten

Belonging to the same family as the stoat and weasel, the pine marten resembles other members of this family in general body shape. Indeed, at first sight one might be forgiven for thinking that it is an overgrown stoat! There is a wide variety of coat colour: darker species are almost black on the upper and under surfaces, whereas lighter ones are a deep chestnut brown. The typical creamy-white patch, common to other weasels, is prominent on the pine marten.

At one time the animal was found over much of Britain, extending north as far as the Hebridean Islands. Today, its exact distribution is not really known, but it has been reported in the western Highlands, which seem to be its strong-hold, Wales and the Lake District. It has decreased in numbers mainly because its preferred haunt, woodland, has been disappearing. In some places it has moved into areas with sparse cover, particularly in parts of Scotland, where it now survives in rocky terrain, seeking out crevices for cover.

As with so many woodland species, the pine marten has attracted the attention of gamekeepers who have shot it because of its suspected theft of gamebird chicks. Although it might occasionally take some, if the opportunity arises and other food is scarce, such occurrences are rare. Its wide-ranging diet includes berries, as well as carrion, small birds and rodents.

Polecat

The polecat has done more than most other members of the *mustelidae* to earn a bad reputation. Once labelled thus, it became an enemy of all gamekeepers and indiscriminate shooting has led to its downfall and its present rating as an endangered species in Britain.

Because of its low numbers, coupled with the fact that it seeks out areas away from man, its present assumed status is based mainly on guesswork and sporadic sightings. Naturalists are generally agreed that if it does still have a stronghold this is in Wales and along the Welsh borders. Some optimists still claim that it has managed to retain a foothold in the Lake District and in some southwestern counties of England such as Devon and Cornwall.

The polecat is often confused with its close relative, the feral polecat-ferret; this is mainly because people have difficulty in obtaining a good sighting, due to the speed with which the animal moves.

Its territory established, it marks this with a combination of urine and the secretion from an anal gland. The home is made in a variety of situations, ranging from cracks in rocks to disused rabbit burrows. Although it is not very good at climbing, it swims extremely well.

Stealthy watchfulness is no match for the hunter's gun which has accounted for the serious decline in the polecat population. (Eric Hosking)

Left: *Almost extinct, extensive protection measures for the Spanish lynx have probably come too late. This one can be seen in Cologne Zoo.* (Frank Lane)

Spanish Lynx

Various countries have lost species which are still to be found in other areas. When Stone Age Man lived in Britain, one of the animals which shared his homeland was the Spanish lynx. Since then, changes have taken place not only in the human population of the British Isles and Europe, but also in the number and variety of species as well. Fossil records show that this particular lynx was once widespread in western Europe, as well as in the eastern part of North America and in Newfoundland.

The disappearance of large tracts of woodland has meant an end to the Spanish lynx's main habitat. This, coupled with the fact that it was ruthlessly hunted by man because of the danger caused to his domestic stock, has made it one of the world's rarest mammals.

Today the Spanish species of lynx has been eradicated in most places, except for areas where it is now protected. These protection methods have probably come too late, and there are probably less than twenty pairs which now inhabit the Spanish Donana National Park. In the wild it makes a lair in a wide variety of places, including burrows and bushes, and sometimes in the disused nests of birds such as storks, as high as 15m (45ft) off the ground.

In spite of the animal's great agility, it has not escaped man's onslaught and it seems likely that its fate is sealed and its extinction is but a matter of time.

Below: *A lynx stalking prey in Spain's Donana National Park.*

Wild Cat

At first glance one could be excused for thinking that the wild cat is a domestic tabby. Further acquaintance will soon show a number of marked differences, most noticeable of which is probably its body size. The body is both larger and broader than the domestic cat, and the thick, fluffy tail stands out because of the bands of light and dark fur which encircle it.

The wild cat, still found over much of Europe, was probably once a common species over much of Britain. Today its range is more protracted and it occurs only on the Scottish mainland. Where the Forestry Commission has planted large tracts of coniferous woodland this has provided a suitable haunt for the wild cat.

Its territory varies and includes moorland, coniferous plantations and rocky outcrops. Its den may be in an abandoned nest, in a cave, or perhaps in a tree stump. Although the area which it quarters for food usually covers just under 80 hectares (200 acres), it will range over a much wider area if food is scarce.

The fact that the wild cat has been hunted over a long period of time has almost certainly led to its decline. Its habits have not endeared it to farmers and gamekeepers, especially where it attacks and kills lambs and game birds.

Below: *When aggressive, the wild cat cannot be mistaken for the domestic tabby.* (NSP, G. Kinns)

Otter

It is perhaps strange that such a beautifully streamlined swimmer should be in danger. That is, until one looks more closely at the otter's way of life. Most of the food which the animal eats consists of fish and it has suffered as a result of this. In order to preserve the stock of fish in rivers, the otter has been hunted by sportsmen to such an extent that its distribution is sparse. Realising that the animal is in danger, the British government has passed legislation to protect it from its human hunters.

A member of the weasel family, with a lithe body characteristic of the group, it has evolved in such a way that it is well equipped for a life in water. With a powerful tail, webbed feet, streamlined body and dense fur, the otter is particularly well adapted for this mode of life.

Although the otter is widespread over much of Britain, its population tends to be greater where there are good lengths of waterway. It is more likely to be seen, for example, in the river system of eastern England. Here Philip Wayre, owner and director of the Norfolk Wildlife Park, has established the Otter Trust near Bungay in Suffolk.

Because of its aquatic habits it seldom strays far from water and will be found in marshes, lakes, rivers and streams, as well as along the coast where suitable food is available. Otters which have been seen well away from water have usually been moving from one river system to another.

Very little is known about the mammal's life history in the wild, although much information has been collected from captive species. It has been suggested that there is only one litter a year, which consists of two or three cubs.

Right: *Standing proud and alert on the river bank, this once common view of the otter is now rare.* (OSF)

Common or Hazel Dormouse

To almost everyone in Europe the dormouse is *the* mouse — and the one animal which typifies a hibernatory species. It is surprising therefore that this small mammal has become rare, particularly in Britain. Although termed *common,* this attribute is one which should be abandoned, and even the alternative name of hazel dormouse is somewhat misleading. The latter, rather than referring to its colour, was used to indicate the animal's distribution at one time — it occurred mainly in hazel woods.

The decrease in the dormouse population is probably due in the main to the loss of its habitat, most hazel woodlands having been chopped down. It has also been suggested that the grey squirrel has moved into areas which the dormouse inhabits, with the result that the smaller mammal has been driven out. If this is so, the reason for such a conflict is not known.

Another factor which should be considered is that while the animal is hibernating through the winter months, it is particularly vulnerable to other animals out in search of a meal. Experts have suggested that in some areas only a third of the animals which start the winter's sleep will survive and be ready to breed in the following year.

Enjoying a meal of hawthorn berries, the large eyes of the dormouse give an indication of its nocturnal habits. (Heather Angel)

Peregrine Falcon

About the size of a pigeon, the peregrine falcon is a typical bird of prey. Its status varies from country to country but in Britain, for example, it is a specially protected bird. During the sixties and early seventies it suffered greatly from the effects of highly toxic pesticides used on the land. Although the animals on which the peregrine fed did not die from these poisons, the peregrine did. Some adults may have been killed by the effects of the poisons and in many cases the females' eggs which were laid were found to be infertile.

Because the majority of the breeding sites of the peregrine are inaccessible, being situated on rocky cliff ledges, they are relatively safe from human predators. Although most birds make their own nests, occasionally they will occupy one deserted by some other bird, such as a raven. Found on high ground, the bird occurs in scattered areas of Wales and western England, as well as in larger numbers in northern England and Scotland.

It seems likely that the major part of the peregrine's diet consists of medium-sized birds, a preference for pigeons being particularly noted; sea birds also feature in the food supply. In most areas smaller mammals are also taken, the maximum size being that of a rabbit. With extremely good eyesight, the bird will dive from considerable heights in a headlong swoop, striking and capturing the prey at great speed.

At the height of the pesticide disaster in Britain, the number of pairs went down from 700 to 100. Now that there is a ban on certain very toxic chemicals, the bird seems to be on the increase.

Left and below: *Blessed with very good eyesight, the peregrine falcon will swoop from a height to capture its prey.* (NHPA, E. Murtomäki; Bio-Arts, D. Burn)

Sparrowhawk

Like so many other birds of prey, the sparrowhawk was particularly affected by the use of poisonous sprays in agriculture during the sixties. Its decline has given rise to a great deal of alarm to naturalists. Although found over a large area, it never occurs in large numbers. Like some other birds of prey, it is protected by government laws which, to some degree, make it less vulnerable to man's activities than some other species.

Its nesting site selected, it will build a structure from sticks in a copse or wood, using the higher branches of a conifer tree for this purpose. It will lay a clutch of four to six eggs in May, and these will hatch out about twenty-four days later. Generally, it only has one brood per year so that if there is a bad season, the population will decline.

The sparrowhawk takes both birds and mammals and, where the supply is plentiful, it will show a preference for song birds. These are supplemented by small mammals, including voles, mice and rats.

Below: *Guarding nestlings, the fate of the sparrowhawk seems to be more secure now that many toxic pesticides are no longer used so extensively.* (NHPA)

Spanish or Imperial Eagle

No one will deny that the Spanish eagle is anything less than a majestic bird. Although it seems to have begun to decline in numbers during the 20th century, it is likely that its fate had been sealed more than 100 years ago. Yet fossil remains indicate that this eagle has existed for many centuries. Unlike many other endangered species, which breed quite easily in captivity, birds of prey do not respond well when kept in cages.

Today, as its name implies, it is probably now confined to Spain; it is likely that the Coto Donana is its sole breeding ground. Although this important area is a nature reserve, it is very difficult to patrol successfully, although wardening is now improving. Hopefully, therefore, the Spanish eagle will increase in numbers, although whether it manages to re-colonise its earlier range, which used to include Portugal, Morocco and Algeria, is purely speculative.

It is particularly because of its flesh-eating activities that man has made the bird a target for slaughter. Although the food taken only consists of wild species, such as rabbits, hares, reptiles and carrion, man has assumed that his livestock will also be taken.

Above: *A Spanish eagle at the nest.* (NHPA, B. Hawkes)

Lammergeier

Although the lammergeier is found in Africa, where it is rare, it can also be found in Europe. The African lammergeier has the alternative name of the bearded vulture. In stature the bird is perhaps more closely akin to the eagle than the vulture. Its behaviour also has little in common with the vulture.

One of its interesting habits is bone dropping, which has been recorded for posterity for many generations. Pliny, the Roman writer, recorded how the poet Aeschylus died as the result of being hit by a tortoise which a lammergeier had dropped. The poet was unfortunately bald and, according to the story, the bird must have mistaken the hairless part of the man's anatomy for a stone!

Recent accounts have shown that the bird intentionally drops bones from a great height onto hard surfaces in order to shatter them. Once the bone has broken, the lammergeier eats the nutritious marrow which is inside. Perhaps it is not surprising, therefore, that the natives of Spain have dubbed it the 'guebrantahuesos', which means 'bone-breaker'.

It is undoubtedly because of its bone-dropping habits that it has been accused of a wide variety of crimes, including the snatching of large animals and human babies. The truth of the matter is that, because the ends of its talons are blunt, it would find it extremely difficult to grasp large objects.

The decrease in the number of lammergeiers is partly due to the long period needed for the female to reach maturity. It is further aggravated by the fact that the female, having reached maturity, only lays one egg at a time, so leaving little room for failure. Poisons too, have led to the bird's downfall.

Left: *Known alternatively as the bearded vulture, the lammergeier is found in Africa as well as Europe.* (Eric Hosking)

Audouin's Gull

At one time gulls were synonymous with the coastline, but now they have spread to many other habitats, and have taken advantage of man as the provider of food. In some areas, gulls seem to be as numerous inland as they are around the coast; others live by inland lakes and reservoirs, and have probably never seen the sea.

Although it is likely that Audouin's gull was quite common at the beginning of this century, it has never been widespread. Naturalists are of the opinion that it has always been restricted to an area bordering the Mediterranean.

Although many of the more common gull species have increased both their numbers and territories, Audouin's gull has decreased dramatically. The exact reason for its decline is not known, but its shy and cautious manner may well have contributed.

A recent survey has indicated that, although the number of birds is not very great, it may be more widespread than was originally thought. Its habit of shunning man may account for the earlier reports of its decrease. One pressing threat lies in the destruction of its eggs. Some are taken for food, others by predators, and yet more by collectors.

Below: *Audouin's gulls, which are thought to be restricted to the Mediterranean.* (Ardea Photographics)

Indian or Asian Elephant

With the destruction of its habitat, large numbers of the Indian elephant have disappeared. Although it is still found in the countries which are usually associated with this species, the population in all areas has declined; herds have diminished in size, and become more scattered. Present estimations suggest that the world population in the wild has fallen below 20,000 animals and this is causing great concern to naturalists.

It is perhaps somewhat misleading to refer to the animal as the Indian elephant since it also occurs in other countries, including Ceylon, Burma, Malaya, Borneo, Sumatra, Thailand and Laos.

Although undisputedly a very large animal, it is its relative, the African elephant, which claims the record as the largest surviving land mammal. Even so, the Asian species is quite large enough, and a fully grown bull can reach 4035kg (5 tons). A tape measure placed around an animal's leg would probably read out at up to 1.5m (5ft). The most obvious difference between the two species is that the Asian elephant possesses smaller ears than the African.

The elephant has served man for many centuries and, as far as the Asiatic species is concerned, the rules for domesticating the species are contained in an old Assamese book, *Hastividyarnava*.

Pages 42 & 43: *Indian elephants at the water's edge.* (Ardea Photographics, J. Ferrero)

Below: *A herd of Indian elephants. Note the ears which are much smaller than the African variety.* (Aquila Photographics, N. Jagannathan)

Przewalski's Horse

At one time many species of wild horse roamed the earth, as witnessed by the numerous fossil remains which have been uncovered. All but one of these has become extinct, the sole survivor being Przewalski's horse which is the only truly wild horse in existence in the 20th century.

No one is really certain whether any still survive in the wild, and an added blow came in the severe winter of 1962-3 when it seems likely that many which occured in Mongolia perished in the long period of extremely low temperatures. Today, any wild stock which remains probably occupies inhospitable country in the west of Mongolia, as well as in the Altai mountains.

Many zoos have had considerable breeding successes with Przewalski's horse, and today there are probably more than 300 in captivity.

Above: *The last surviving species of the wild horse, it is probable that Przeswalski's horse is now extinct in the wild.* (NHPA, Philippa Scott)

Pere David's Deer

Although there are many herds of Pere David's deer in various collections throughout the world, the animal has become extinct in the wild state. Once it must have been a common sight to see the deer move gracefully across the plains of northeast China. But that was long ago, for it became extinct in the wild during the Shang Dynasty which came to an end in 1122 BC. Fortunately, many herds had already been established in parks, and it is in these groups that it has survived.

When the famous French naturalist Pere David visited China in 1865, he had the nerve to look over the wall of one of the country's parks, a place which was banned to Europeans. He was intrigued by what he saw, for there was a deer which he did not know. He managed to obtain two skins and later some live animals which were given to various zoos.

Pere David's actions were indeed timely, for a few years later the walls of the park were breached by flood water and the deer escaped, most of them being killed by the peasants. All but a few which survived this disaster died during a rebellion at the turn of the century. Those which lived were taken to Peking, but were dead by 1911.

The Duke of Bedford set up a herd at Woburn Abbey in England and eventually, after many breeding successes, animals were sent back to China.

Below: *Although extinct in the wild, herds of Pere David's deer can be seen in captivity in various parts of the world.* (Eric Hosking)

Arabian Oryx

Having the distinction of being hunted and caged by the Ancient Egyptians, and so managing to survive for several centuries, the Arabian oryx is now an extinct species in the wild. Breeding successes in captivity have been good, and some of these animals are being released into selected areas in the wild. It is by this careful conservation programme that the animal has not become totally extinct.

Before the advent of modern firearms and fast vehicles, the method of taking an oryx was to pursue it either on foot or on the back of a camel. Because the animals were able to compete with man and camel, many managed to escape. So the numbers which were killed in this way each year were relatively small. Not so today — while it was possible for the oryx to survive against man and his camel, it had little chance against the powerful gun and the motor vehicle.

Once an animal had been captured, there were few parts of the body which did not have their uses, and whether some of the claims are true or false, modern man still pursued and captured large numbers. The meat was valued on two counts. It had a particularly good flavour and the local people also considered that the animal's fleetness of foot would be transferred to man on eating the meat.

The fact that the Arabian oryx managed to survive for so long was due to the personal intervention of the Muscat of Oman, who was particularly interested in the species. But even his power was not great enough to keep out raiding parties which came over the border with fast vehicles and powerful guns.

Right: *Successful breeding in captivity has saved the Arabian oryx from extinction. None exist in the wild.* (Bruce Coleman Ltd.)

Orang-utan

It is strange that such a well-known, if not well-loved animal, should be so rare. And yet such is the case with the orang-utan or 'forest-man' in the Malay tongue. Its last stronghold, if that term can be allowed when referring to a threatened species, is in the tropical forests of the large islands of Sumatra and Borneo, in the Indian Ocean. Of the great apes, the orang-utan is the only species which is to be found outside central Africa. Skeletal remains, discovered in many other places, indicate that the species was much more widespread than today's population suggests.

Adapted for a life in the trees, its long arms enable the orang-utan to swing easily from one branch to another. Yet in spite of this adaptation, its movements are precise, slow and deliberate, as if it needs to calculate its every move very carefully. To see it moving in this deliberate way does, to some extent, belie the fact that when the occasion arises it has a remarkable turn of speed.

Committed to a family life style, it is only the old males which lead a solitary existence. Whether they have been rejected by a family group, or whether they have chosen to live independently, is a matter for conjecture.

The decline in numbers is due in the main to the earlier demands made by zoological societies. To be successful in captivity, it was assumed that youngsters were needed, but to capture one of these it usually meant that the female had to be killed. Once in captivity, the young orangs were often fed incorrect diets and death resulted. Capture usually proved easy for although large, with an adult weighing 90kg (200lb), they are not difficult to take as they apparently show little sign of fear or anger.

Left & below: *The orang-utan, the old man of the forests, may only be found in its wild state on the islands of Sumatra and Borneo.* (NHPA, P. Wayre; Frank Lane)

Giant Panda

The apparently charming nature of the giant panda has endeared the mammal to the public at large. The first pandas were discovered in 1869, when Pere David, a noted French naturalist, made an expedition to China. Although one can be forgiven for assuming that the panda is a bear — and at first it was classified as such — it is in fact related to kinkajous and racoons.

Today, as far as is known, its only habitat is in bamboo forests on the Chuing-lai mountains, in the Szechwan region of China. Because it is very difficult to study the animal in the wild state, very little is known about it and the only information which has been collected has come from those which have been kept captive in zoos, notably from London, Peking, and Moscow. The public imagination has recently identified with the giant panda during various exchanges in which attempts have been made to mate the species in captivity. Breeding in captivity had only been successful at Peking Zoo.

Now protected by the Chinese government, it seems that the animals may be on the increase, in spite of natural predators such as the leopard and wild dog. Solitary by nature, those in captivity, like London's Chia Chia and Ching Ching, are kept apart for much of the time.

Left: *The giant panda, which inhabits remote bamboo forests in China, is now protected by legislation.* (S. C. Bisserot)

Snow Leopard

If many of the other wild cats in Asia are on the very edge of extinction, then such a statement is also sadly true of the magnificent snow leopard. Indeed, many authorities consider it to be the rarest of the threatened cat species. Unfortunately it is also the one species about which very little information has been accumulated.

In remote countryside it is often difficult to enforce laws which are aimed at protecting wild species. In Nepal, in spite of the theoretical protection, the snow leopard is still hunted in such a way that extinction must be very close. Although considered at its most common on the slopes of the Himalayan mountains, where it generally favours higher ground above the timber line, even here it is rarely encountered.

Although local hunters manage to track and kill the animal, often using poison arrows, there is still much to be learned about the animal's life history.

Such is the difficult nature of the leopard's habitat that man is either not prepared, or not able, to make intensive studies in an inhospitable climate. It is known that the animal is nocturnal and this, coupled with its secretive habits, makes study particularly difficult.

Although there is an ever-decreasing call for the fur of the snow leopard, the local people still continue to hunt it, probably because this is a way of life which has become inbred, and so is difficult to eradicate. This, together with the fact that not only is it rare, but difficult to kill, makes the snow leopard a particularly prized species. Indeed, to catch one is a means of showing a hunter's particular skills and prowess — a kind of one-upmanship against his fellows.

Death to the wild cat usually comes accidentally. Musk and blue sheep are also hunted by the local tribesmen who kill them by setting poison spears in the ground. Although meant for the other species, snow leopards will die if they come upon the poisoned spears.

Right & below: *Very little is known about the snow leopard which, sadly, is on the verge of extinction.* (Bruce Coleman Ltd, N. Tomalin and G. Schaller)

Asiatic Lion

As well as the familiar African lion, there is also a species which is found in Asia. To distinguish between the two is a task for an expert, and even then there is no universal agreement. As there are always differences between individuals, classification is often difficult. However, according to naturalists the differences between the African and Asiatic species are discovered by looking at the mane and tail. In the Asiatic lion, the tassel which is found at the end of the tail is reputedly longer, and the mane not so thick.

The decline in the numbers of Asiatic lions has only been quite recent, as humans have taken over areas which were the lion's domain. Today, the animal which once roamed much of Asia Minor, Arabia, Persia and India is now confined to the Gir Sanctuary (Gujarat State) in India. Although the animal has had as much protection there as has been possible, its population has fluctuated over the years: no one seems to know why, although one possible explanation is that there has been a decrease in the wild food supply. Still having to survive, the lion often resorted to domestic animals but the local inhabitants, understandably unhappy, put down poison bait to deter their predations. Its normal diet consists of wild pigs, nilgai, chital and sambas.

Lions live in family groups known as prides. These units usually consist of an average of ten animals. It is the male, once dubbed 'King of the Forest', which is bedecked with the majestic mane. Larger than the female, he may weigh in excess of 180kg (400lb), and have a total length of 2.4m (8ft), including the tail.

Left: *The Asiatic lion on the prowl for food is often the victim of poison bait.* (NHPA, E. H. Rao)

Above: *Killed for its fur, the numbers of Siberian tigers have decreased dramatically to the point of extinction.* (Animals Animals, A. Thomas)

Siberian or Manchurian Tiger

Just as fashions change, so do man's attitudes to some of the world's wild species, particularly once they are studied and more information is known about their life history. Such is the case of the Siberian (or Manchurian) tiger. At one time the Chinese regarded it as a pest: now they are doing their utmost to conserve this rare species.

In addition to its downfall as a supposed pest, it was also killed for its fine fur. Many animals also undoubtedly died because of a locally held belief that its bones had medicinal properties. This was a legend which must have been handed down from one family to the next for many generations. Because of the nature of the area in which the tiger lives, exact numbers are difficult to come by, but estimates suggest that there are probably no more than a few hundred left in the wild.

Found in northeast China, Korea and Siberia, there are also specimens in zoos throughout the world. Its natural Asian home is a far cry from Britain's Marwell Zoological Park (Winchester, Hampshire), where there is an extremely thriving breeding herd. Estimates have shown that with this group, and others in captivity throughout the world, there are nearly 700 Siberian tigers surviving in collections.

Swinhoe's Pheasant

In contrast to the many stories of species in decline, there are also some which show success. One of these concerns Swinhoe's pheasant. Philip Wayre, founder of the Norfolk Wildlife Park in England, was also responsible for establishing the Ornamental Pheasant Trust, the purpose of which was to breed endangered species of pheasants.

Named after the British naturalist Swinhoe, who discovered the pheasant in 1862, this beautifully marked bird was in serious danger in the wild state. A bird confined to the hill forests of Formosa, little was known about it and the countryside which it occupied. Vast numbers of trees have been felled in the area in order to make way for a rapidly expanding population and to provide natural materials for industry. The result was that the pheasant was left with an ever-decreasing habitat.

With the success of the breeding campaign at the Ornamental Pheasant Trust, birds have now been taken back to Formosa with the hope that they will again breed naturally and build up a reasonable wild population. In spite of these efforts, the bird is still not out of danger; but conservation measures in its natural homeland, and breeding successes in Britain, will help to alleviate a situation in which the bird was on the verge of extinction.

Below: *Due to successful breeding techniques in captivity, a number of Swinhoe's pheasants have been returned to their original homeland of Formosa.* (Eric Hosking)

Africa

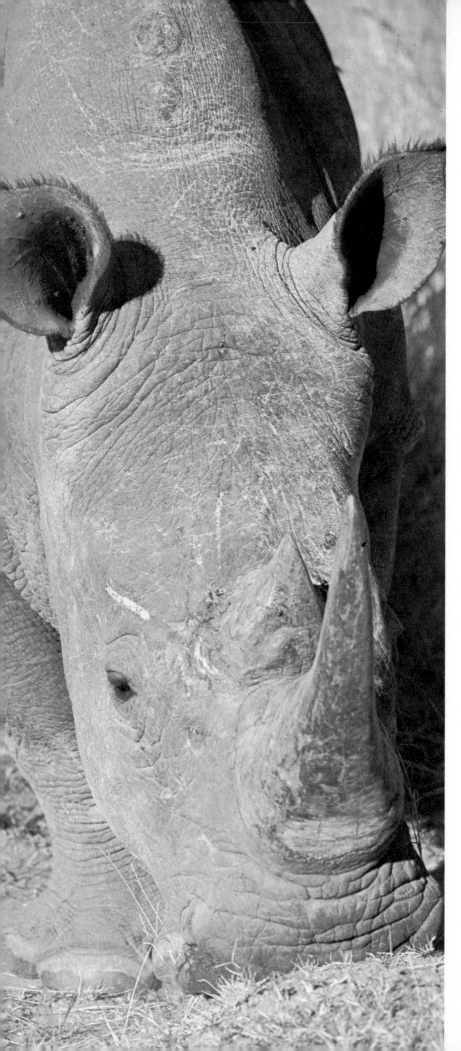

White Rhinoceros

Although commonly called the white rhinoceros, it is more accurate to refer to this species as the 'square-lipped' rhinoceros, for the name 'white' is a corruption of the Dutch word *wijd* which means 'square-lipped'.

Occupying its own particular niche on the African continent, the square-lipped rhino had a far greater range in earlier times than it occupies today. A grazing animal, it will be found in an area south of the vast Sahara desert, as long as there is grassland on which it can feed.

By far the largest population of these massive animals — a fully-grown individual may weigh over 3050kg (3 tons) — used to be found in the Garamba National Park, and although a number were killed by raiders, the population in the Park was not disastrously affected. The situation changed, however, when hostilities began in the mid-sixties and large numbers were killed. Prior to these activities, it was estimated that the Park contained a population slightly in excess of 1000; within a short time only a hundred or so remained.

Although its 'armour-plating' gives an impression that the rhino is both fearsome and cumbersome, it is generally docile by nature and very easy to approach. It was the introduction of modern weapons, coupled with loss of habitat, that put the status of the animal in jeopardy.

There are a number of herds in captivity, including a large one at Whipsnade Zoo Park in Bedfordshire, England, and it is hoped that, as with some other species, it will be possible to return them to their natural habitat in due course.

Pages 58 & 59: *White rhino with young, grazing.*

Left: *The special lip structure of the white rhino enables it to crop grass very closely.* (NHPA, P. Johnson)

Mountain Gorilla

The mountain gorilla, inhabiting inaccessible countryside in West Africa, was first recorded in 1947. Many animals have acquired reputations which are undeserved and inaccurate. Perhaps it is to be expected that an animal of such proportions — an adult male may weigh in excess of 180kg (400lb) — created a legend of having a particularly fierce character. Such a reputation remained with the gorilla for a little over one hundred years. It was only when George Schaller and his wife lived with groups of these animals for a year and a half that they were able to dispel the stories and give a true picture of the animal; this dramatically altered the reputation with which it had previously been credited.

The mountain gorilla suffers from a poor rate of reproduction. It is reckoned that a single young is born to a female only once every four years. A young gorilla stays with the female for about three years and only when the youngster becomes independent will the female become pregnant again. If a female is deprived of her offspring, mating will take place more frequently.

Added to these problems, the mountain gorilla has been subjected to the onslaught of hunters and it is certainly unlikely that the species will increase its numbers in the wild. Using different methods of capture, including pitfall traps and snares, the tribesmen kill the animal for food. Earlier too, when it was fashionable to collect species, many collectors destroyed large numbers of adults in order to take the young. The mountain gorilla will only be effectively protected if stringent conservation methods can be enforced.

Below: *Killed for food and captured for many zoological collections, the mountain gorilla is now in great danger of becoming another extinct species.* (Eric Hosking)

Aye Aye

First discovered in 1780, the aye aye is the only survivor of its particular family. Now found on Madagascar, where it is confined to coastal forests in the north-eastern part of the island, there are no reliable estimates of the animal's numbers. This lack of information is due mainly to the inaccessible and difficult nature of the terrain. It seems likely that less than one hundred animals still survive. If this is correct, the aye aye is indeed one of the world's rarest mammals, and is likely to vanish from the face of the earth in the near future.

A strange animal, the aye aye is not unlike a squirrel in body size, although here the comparison ends. Its most interesting feature is undoubtedly its hands which have a long and thin third 'talon'. It is this and the long teeth, rather like those possessed by rodents, which gives a clue to the animal's diet.

It has been suggested that most of the aye aye's food consists of the larvae of wood-boring insects. Credited with a good sense of both smell and hearing, the animal uses these to seek out its food. The middle finger is then employed to remove the larvae from the wood, once the large teeth have torn at the timber.

Its large eyes are a particularly valuable asset. At the best of times, light is at a premium in its forest home, but its life-style dictates that it sleeps by day and eats at night, moving from tree to tree, making keen eyesight imperative.

Below: *Living and feeding in the trees, the large eyes of the aye aye are a particular asset in this type of habitat.* (Bruce Coleman Ltd, N. Myers)

Indris

With a range which limits its distribution to the island of Madagascar, as with other island-dwelling species, the indris is in danger of extinction. As the natural forest has been chopped down to increase the land available for agriculture, and to provide wood for the increasing population, the indris, which was once considered an abundant species, has rapidly declined to the stage where it is considered an endangered animal. It has become particularly vulnerable because it only occupies relatively small localised areas in forests along the east coast of the island.

Equipped with extremely powerful hind limbs, the indris clings like a limpet to upright branches of trees, suddenly making a leap to an adjacent bough. Having a diet consisting mainly of vegetable matter, the indris take a wide range of flowers, fruits, nuts and seeds. Although considered to be a tree-living species, where it is obviously at home moving agiley from one branch to another, it does spend time on the ground.

Once considered sacred by the local tribesmen, it was immune from man's activities. According to a locally held tradition, should a tribesman aim his spear at the indris, it would catch it, and return it to the thrower. Today the people of Madagascar are less prone to these pagan ideas than their ancestors and the indris no longer carries a 'sacred' label.

Right: *At home in the trees, the indris has lost great areas of its natural habitat as forests have been chopped down by man.* (Heather Angel)

Barbary Leopard

As man made inroads into various parts of the world, he generally upset the natural state which prevailed before he arrived. The barbary leopard was one of the many animals to suffer. When man started to clear new areas, various species were driven out. The reasons for this are many, but one is generally common: the main source of food for species like the barbary leopard went as well.

Faced with a shortage of food, the mammal naturally turned its attention to the only alternative; it attacked domestic animals. As far as the owners of such domestic species were concerned, the leopard became an enemy and was relentlessly hunted.

Such a situation would probably not have led to a threat of extinction, but this was not all. Leopard skin became a prized and fashionable possession and large numbers of animals have fallen victim to the hunters' weapons, even though such an activity is illegal. With this onslaught, numbers have decreased dramatically, and within a very short time it seems likely that the animals will be added to the ever-increasing list of extinct species.

Right: *Seen resting in the branches of a tree, the barbary leopard is in serious danger as man has moved into its territory.* (Eric Hosking)

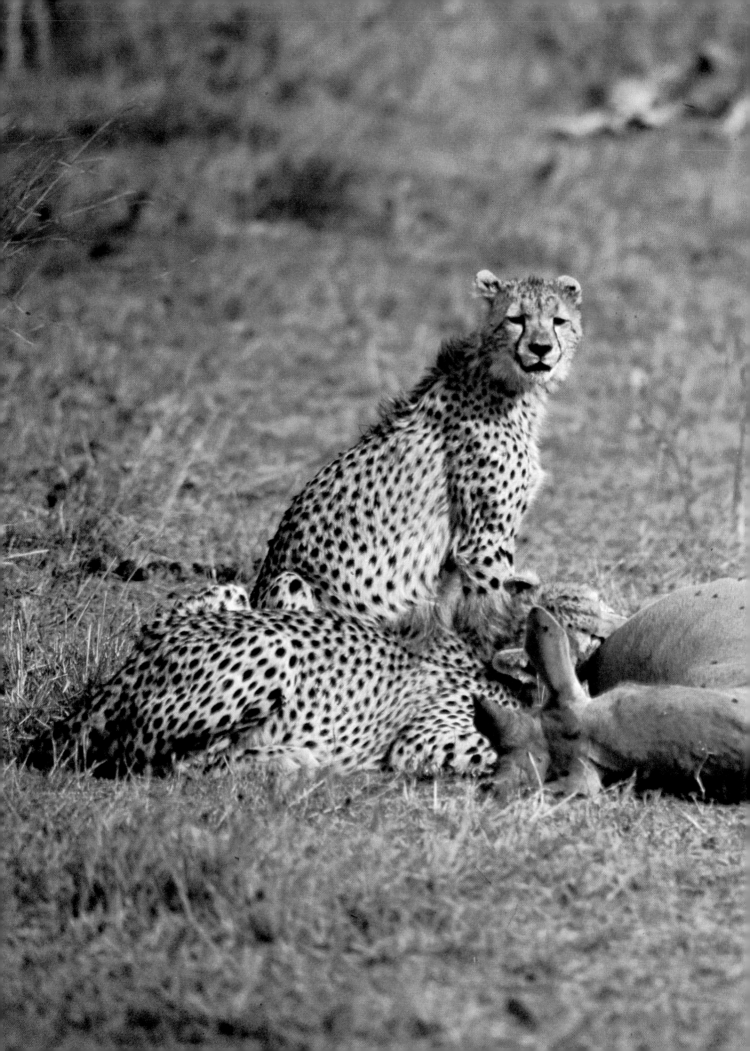

Cheetah

Fleet of foot, graceful and credited with being the fastest of all land animals, the cheetah has, like other species of wild cat, been on the decline for many years now. Like so many other species, its fur was, and still is, highly sought after in some parts of the world. But this alone has not been responsible for its downfall. As man has impinged on the wild animal's natural home, the cheetah has posed a threat to both his livestock and his livelihood.

Although many countries have banned the export of cheetah skin, poaching is still a problem, especially since the pelt is an extremely valuable commodity. Whipsnade Zoo Park in Bedfordshire, England, has certainly done a great deal to help breed the cheetah, and their success rate is one which is much envied by other establishments. No fewer than forty-seven young have been born in a period of ten years.

Left: *Cheetahs at Hartebeest kill.* (Eric Hosking)

Below: *A cheetah with its cub, aged nine weeks.* (NSP, G. Kinns)

Right: *Killed by local tribesmen, and attacked by an infectious disease, the giant eland has been on the decline for several years.* (Frank Lane, E. H. Nightingale)

Western Giant Eland

The giant eland has suffered on two fronts in recent years. The increased number which have been killed by local tribesmen has reduced the population, but by far the most significant threat to the animal has been the effect of under-pest. This infectious disease appeared towards the end of the 19th century, and since then several epidemics have quickly spread across Africa attacking the antelopes, including the eland. Domestic cattle have also suffered greatly from the disease. In certain parts of the continent, where cattle have been immunised against the disease, the eland seems to be in a much better position than in areas where such a programme has not been carried out.

Addax

In the past, the addax was found over a much wider area than it is today. It is now found in a hostile region of the western Sahara desert. So barren is this wilderness that although animals like the addax manage to survive, man has found the conditions intolerable, for not only is there no protection from the elements, but there is also very little water or food.

One of the rarest of the antelopes, over the years the addax has evolved in such a way that it is able to tolerate extremely difficult conditions. For this very reason, many naturalists consider it to be unique. Confined to life in this desert region, the animal does not take water, but gets enough liquid from the desert plants which it eats. Yet even these are very sparse, appearing only when the region is subjected to an occasional downpour. The addax's livelihood demands an inborn instinct which enables it to find these patches of vegetation and so it often travels considerable distances in its search for food.

Local tribesmen on camels make regular sorties into the inhospitable desert region to capture and kill the addax. While these probably have little effect on the antelope's population, the same cannot be said for the modern hunter with his sophisticated transport and firearms.

Offered protection by law, it is highly unlikely that the legislation can be administered effectively, due to the nature of the terrain in which it lives.

Right: An addax in Pretoria Zoo. (Bruce Coleman Ltd, N. Myers)

Rusty Numbat

Although the western numbat, a close relative to the rusty numbat, is in no serious danger, the same cannot be said for the rusty species, which is on the verge of extinction. The animal, once widespread over many Australian states, including Western Australia, Southern Australia and New South Wales, has declined, perhaps even to the point where its fate is irreversible.

According to some conservationists, the reasons for its downfall have been numerous. The introduction of non-native species, including the fox and domestic dog, have increased its death-rate. This is in addition to the clearance of vast tracts of countryside and, with colonisation by man, the increase in bush fires which have trapped and destroyed many species.

Sometimes referred to as the banded anteater, because of the striped nature of its coat and the fact that its favourite food consists of termites, the rusty numbat is one of the few marsupials which comes out to feed during the daytime; most others are nocturnal.

Using its particularly powerful claws, it is soon able to break into termite hills; according to some writers, it has a preference for only one or two species. Once the termites are exposed, the animal quickly flicks them into its mouth with its long tongue.

Leadbeater's Possum

There was great rejoicing in naturalist circles when, in 1961, Leadbeater's possum was rediscovered after it had previously been pronounced extinct. After an animal believed to be a Leadbeater's possum was seen in 1961, and later confirmed, other sightings came in, although the animal has never been seen in any numbers.

Preferring areas with Eucalyptus trees, which is where the sightings were made, the animal is believed to give birth to two young at a time which are carried in its pouch, the animal being a marsupial. Very little is known about the possum's behaviour, although it is thought that it makes its nest in old trees which have holes in them.

It is believed that the possum's diet consists mainly of insects. Such an assumption has been made because of the way in which the animal reacted in captivity, refusing to eat nuts, fruit, leaves, and even raw meat, but readily taking insects.

Remains of owl pellets, found in areas in which Leadbeater's possum used to live, showed that there were remains of the possum when the pellets were dissected. However, newer pellets showed a decreasing amount of possum remains, which suggests that as the animals have decreased in numbers, owls have had to make do with other animals.

Pages 70 & 71: *The rusty numbat, unlike most marsupials, feeds by day, having a preference for termites.* (NHPA, F. Baglin)

Right: *Previously thought to be extinct, Leadbeater's possum was rediscovered in 1961.* (NHPA)

Hairy-nosed Wombat

Once found over a large area of Australia, the hairy-nosed wombat is now in serious decline. Only found in scattered colonies in the southern part of the island, conservationists are worried about its future.

A nocturnal marsupial, it takes only vegetable matter, including the bark of some trees, roots of various plants and a wide variety of leaves. It has no problem when digging up roots as it uses its very strong claws which are well adapted for this purpose.

Measuring almost a metre (39in) in length, the hairy-nosed wombat is small when compared to some of its fossil relatives which have been discovered. These include such extinct forms as *Dioprotodon* and *Nototherium*. Apparently these species favoured damper conditions, and while some of their predecessors managed to adapt to living in drier situations, others became extinct. They were unable to adapt to changing environmental conditions.

Wombats have features which are common to rodents. Because they are gnawing animals, they have two pairs of large incisors; one in the upper and one in the lower jaw. Like rodents, the teeth do not have roots and continue to grow, replacing the parts which wear away.

Left: *Nocturnal by nature, the hairy-nosed wombat has decreased in recent years.* (Bruce Coleman Ltd, J. Wallis)

Native Cat

Although not particularly cat-like, either by nature or habit, the native cat has probably derived its name from its size, which is more or less akin to that of a domestic tabby.

Although it is likely that this species will manage to survive for some time, particularly as new conservation measures have been introduced, its numbers have decreased dramatically. Once found over a wide area of Australia, its distribution is now confined to small pockets, mainly in the southeastern part of the country, as well as on the large off-shore island of Tasmania.

Like many 'true' cats, the hours of daylight are spent sleeping, usually in holes, either in or under trees, among rocks or in caves. It will come out at dusk to stalk and kill small mammals, including rabbits, rats and mice. As poultry are easy game, it will also take these when the opportunity arises.

Right: *Feeding on a dead parrot, the native cat is nocturnal in habit, sleeping by day and feeding at night.* (NHPA, M. Morcombe)

Ground Parrot

As long ago as the beginning of the present century, it was thought that the ground parrot had already become extinct. And yet only a few years before, it had been considered quite common, especially along a strip of land bordering the coastlines between Australia and Tasmania.

No nests were seen between 1913 and 1940. But a sighting was made in 1952, and further reports in the 1960s gave fresh hope that the bird was still alive. Now the bird is fully protected by legislation.

Takahe

Now confined to the South Island of New Zealand, the takahe was first described, not from a live bird, but from various fossil remains which were found. Once also inhabiting New Zealand's North Island, it probably became extinct there at the end of the 19th century.

It was not until a group of men set out in 1948 to look specifically for, and eventually discover, the takahe, that the world knew it was still living. Because of its rarity, within a short time of its rediscovery the New Zealand Government made the area where the bird lived into a nature reserve. It occurs on mountain sides at heights varying from 1000-1150m (3300-3800ft) above sea-level.

In spite of the bird's protection, and the fact that its habitat is very difficult to reach — something which undoubtedly favours the continued existence of the takahe — it has declined in numbers. Ornithologists are of the opinion that the birds are for some reason not as fertile as they were, and this is a factor which could eventually lead to their extinction.

A large, almost flightless bird, with a blue head and belly, green back and bright red beak, the takahe is able to get away from would-be attackers with a fast turn of speed.

Left: *Originally thought to be extinct, the ground parrot's status is precarious.* (Ardea Photographics, G. Chapman)

Right: *Almost flightless, the takahe makes its escape by running swiftly.* (Spectrum, H. Axell)

Cape Barren Goose

The Bass Strait, off the western coast of
Australia, has become the home of the
Cape Barren goose. Although one asso-
ciates many species of geese with water,
this particular bird seldom swims.
Mainly an island species, its numbers
have declined off this part of the
Australian coastline.

This is probably due in no small
measure to the fact that the once uninhabited islands have been taken over by
man. As the human population has
moved in to the habitat which was once
the province of the goose, the birds have
turned their attention to man's crops.
Although a protected species, it has been
continually persecuted because of the
damage which it does to growing crops.

Some islands have been declared bird
sanctuaries and others are becoming
uninhabited once again, as the desire for
urbanisation gathers momentum. The
goose does, however, still remain in
danger from the influx of tourists.

Protection is improving and perhaps
this, coupled with the fact that the bird
will nest almost anywhere, may help it to
survive. Although eggs may not be laid
until June, the geese often take up, and
defend, their nesting territory as early as
February. Selecting suitable tussocks of
the grass, the bird will provide a lining
with its own down. Once completed,
between four and seven eggs, ovoid and
white, are laid in the nest.

Right: *As it has lost many of its natural
feeding grounds, the Cape Barren goose has
steadily declined in numbers. This one is to
be found on the island of Flinders, in the
Bass Strait.* (NHPA, D. Baglin)

Oceans &
Islands

Pages 82 & 83 and above: *Despite legislation which is aimed at protecting the walrus, there are still too many animals being killed annually to raise its status beyond a vanishing species.* (Ardea Photographics, E. Jones and P. Morris)

Atlantic Walrus

The Atlantic walrus has long been sought after for its skin, oil and tusks. Whereas the decrease in the numbers of many species has been a recent phenomenon, the decline of the Atlantic walrus started as long ago as the 16th century. Even then it was killed in large numbers. As more modern and efficient equipment was produced, the rate at which the animals were killed increased dramatically. So great was the slaughter that the walrus completely disappeared from many of its former haunts.

Not only was the animal hunted by commercial concerns, but it was also valuable to the Eskimos. It is true that, unlike many of the hunters, they made much more use of numerous parts of the animal. However, this was no consolation and the species continued to decline.

The Atlantic walrus is a wanderer, its movements being linked to the movements of the sea-ice, and its food supply. The animal's diet consists mainly of molluscs, which it dives for. The teeth which are found in the cheek are strong enough to crush the shells of the animals which it catches.

Because of its almost nomadic movements, it is difficult to discover its exact numbers, although it seems likely that Canadian legislation has helped to stabilize the population. In spite of this, the mammal seems in danger of vanishing as too many are killed annually.

Dugong

The fact that the dugong has managed to survive for so long is remarkable, because many factors have undoubtedly led to its decline. It has no particular defence mechanism, although it does have very good hearing; its breeding rate is slow; and it lives close to the shore, where it has undoubtedly been killed for food. The flesh of the dugong is much relished, and this alone has helped it towards the present danger level.

The flesh is not the only part which is useful. Even the teeth have their value. After extracting the upper incisors, the people of Madagascar ground them in order to use the powder as a food preservative. Oil, too, is a valuable extract which is obtained from the blubber — a fully grown female may produce as much as 27 litres (6 gallons). The extract has been employed in many ways, and some aborigines claim that it is the best cure for many respiratory tract disorders. Whether it is more effective than the oil extracted from other animals is a matter for conjecture, except that many locals swear by it.

Large, and seemingly lethargic, the main food of the dugong consists of marine plants. The animal browses through these in a manner which is somewhat reminiscent of a cow!

Below: *Killed for food, the dugong also provides hunters with many other products. So drastic has been the slaughter, that it is now in danger of extinction.* (Bruce Coleman Ltd, A. Power)

Manatee

Not unlike a seal in general body shape, the manatee is much larger in stature. It was these creatures which, partly because of their size, were assumed to be the mermaids which ancient mariners observed.

Today three distinct species exist. Apart from the one which occurs only along the west African coast, there are others inhabiting lengths of the North and South American coastlines. It is, however, the west African species which is at present the most vulnerable. Occurring in the lower reaches of some west African rivers, and in lagoons, the animal, although shy and wary of humans, is nevertheless very susceptible to them.

It is its gentle and almost lethargic nature which, more than anything else, has been responsible for the manatee's downfall. Grazing on seaweed and other marine vegetation, an adult may weigh 225-450kg (500-1000lbs). Once killed, the animal will provide humans with a good supply of meat and a wide variety of other products which make it a prized catch. In addition to its human persecutors, it seems likely that pollution in the area in which it lives has caused the deaths of a number of animals.

Below: *Feeding on marine plants, the manatee is killed for the wide variety of products that the carcase yields. This particular species comes from South America.* (Bruce Coleman Ltd, M. Freeman)

Southern Sea Otter

Perhaps the demise of the southern sea otter is not surprising. Whenever the mammal has been sighted it has seldom been more than 1.6km (one mile) away from the shore, although it rarely takes to the land. Preferring to live where the water is shallow, it was particularly vulnerable as the hunters sought its fur in the 19th century. From being a common species, particularly off the Californian coast, it reached the point at which extinction was an almost foregone conclusion.

Because its pelt was considered so valuable, the rarer it became the greater it was sought after, and the price on the otter's head rose accordingly. It was around the turn of the present century that the last southern sea otter was killed off the Californian coast.

Although in 1910 the United States Government prohibited the killing of

any specimens off the coastline of the United States, it was generally agreed that the animal had already become extinct, its final fate having already been sealed by the hands of the indiscriminate hunters. Fortunately some mammals did manage to survive and in 1938 a number of them were discovered off the Californian coast. With effective protection, the population has steadily increased and, although very slowly, the animal is beginning to colonise the coastline.

Right and below: *Once thought to be extinct off the Californian coast, the southern sea otter is slowly increasing its numbers.* (Frank Lane, S. McCutcheon)

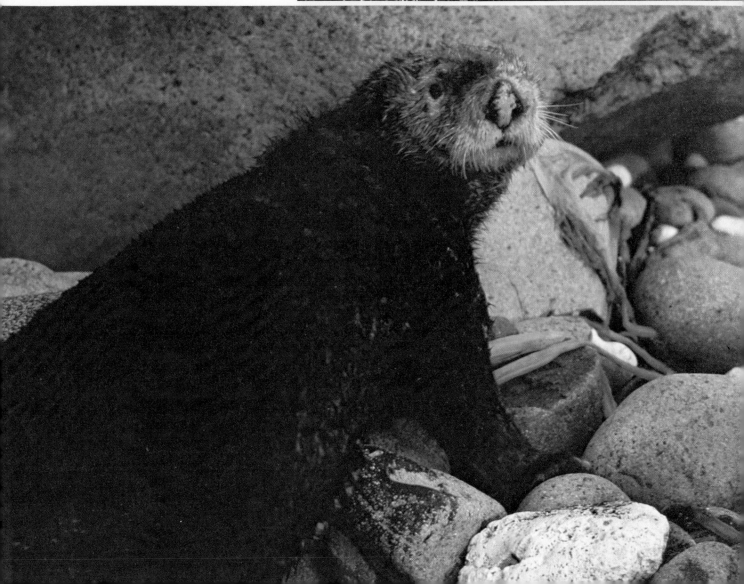

Polar Bear

It is sad to relate that the ever-popular polar bear is suffering the same fate as so many other animals. It is difficult to appreciate that this very familiar mammal occupies one of the most barren areas of the world. This, coupled with its extreme mobility as it moves on the pack ice, ought to deter would-be hunters.

Unfortunately, because the prize is worth having, men have been hunting the polar bear since the sea lanes were first opened in the 17th century. Local people have also turned their attention to hunting, not solely for food, but for a profitable living as well, and the serious decline in the bear's population has become inevitable.

The largest population of polar bears is thought to be in the Canadian Arctic, although it is likely that there are also high numbers in Soviet territory. Certainly the animal's protection is difficult because many of the bears live in international waters, where no one has the necessary legislation to prevent their slaughter. Recently, cooperation has taken place between various countries, and research investigations have been pooled so that, hopefully, the best possible conservation measures can be undertaken.

Right: *At home in the isolated snow-bound wastes, the polar bear has recently been afforded legislative protection from several countries.* (Animals Animals, M. Conte)

Nene (or Hawaiian Goose)

The stories of most animals which have been labelled endangered species have either culminated in their extinction or a failure to increase their numbers satisfactorily. This is not so with the nene or Hawaiian goose.

When the Polynesian settlers arrived on the islands of Hawaii they managed to live in harmony with most of the islands' wildlife, including the nene. It is certain that they hunted it for food, but they probably realised that if they killed too many, their supply would dry up. Sadly, the same cannot be said for the people who arrived from the western world. Almost as soon as they had set foot there, the fate of the nene was sealed. Fortunately, in the 1950s visionaries saw what was happening. With the situation under surveillance, they shipped birds to zoos and private collections and a few survived in Hawaii.

It was the breeding successes of the Wildfowl Trust in Britain which have resulted, at least for the time being, in the threat of extinction being averted. At the Trust's grounds at Slimbridge and Peakirk large numbers of nenes have been bred. Indeed, it has been reckoned that birds in the original Wildfowl Trust nucleus have doubled their numbers each year and many have now been returned to their native land. Now protected, hopefully they will breed successfully to supplement the small numbers which remained.

Below: *Conservation measures, and particularly breeding in captivity, have increased the numbers of the nene, allowing many to be returned to their native islands of Hawaii.* (Bruce Coleman Ltd, L. Dawson)

Right: *Confined to the islands of New Caledonia and Loyalty, the strange kagu was killed for food when settlers arrived in their numbers in the middle of the 19th century.* (Frank Lane)

Kagu

Both New Caledonia Island and Loyalty Island have many unique species of birds. Perhaps it is not surprising when one considers that they are some 1200km (750 miles) from Australia and about the same distance from Fiji. Although the area was first discovered by Captain Cook in 1774, it was when France took possession in 1853 that the first settlers arrived in any numbers. The increasing population has threatened many of the island's birds.

One of the most mysterious of the islands' species is the kagu; scientists have been perpetually puzzled by its lineage. Its exact status was never known for certain although it is assumed that the bird was in no danger when first discovered in 1860. Being large and flightless, it proved easy pickings for the settlers, who caught it by hunting and trapping.

Today, the bird is protected by law and its status is being continually monitored. Although specimens have been sent to many large zoos throughout the world, breeding successes in captivity are extremely rare.

Seychelles Owl

Birds are not the easiest of animals to study. When it comes to owls, the problems increase because they are nocturnal by habit, thus making their identification and tracking doubly difficult. The Seychelles or bare-legged scops owl is no exception to this problem.

Named after the group of islands in the Indian Ocean, today's population is confined to Mahe only. With the exploitation of the Seychelles in recent times, a large number of birds confined to this part of the world have been put at risk, and none more so than the Seychelles owl or 'scieur', as the local inhabitants call it.

It has been suggested that a barn owl, introduced from South Africa, competes for the same food and habitat as the Seychelles owl. If the number of this imported species continues to rise the native owl will become extinct; such a situation is likely to arise in the near future.

So rare and difficult is the bird to observe that very little is known about it. Studies of the bird's size and make up have generally been made from specimens in London's Natural History Museum.

Right: *A particularly rare species, little information has been gathered about the Seychelles owl.* (Eric Hosking)

Index